# SCRATCH CODE CHALLENGE

## Scratch Code
# SPACE TECH

Max Wainewright

CRABTREE PUBLISHING COMPANY
WWW.CRABTREEBOOKS.COM

**CRABTREE**
PUBLISHING COMPANY
WWW.CRABTREEBOOKS.COM

**Author:** Max Wainewright
**Editorial director:** Kathy Middleton
**Editors:** Elise Short, Crystal Sikkens
**Proofreader:** Melissa Boyce
**Design:** Matt Lilly
**Cover design:** Peter Scoulding
**Illustrations:** John Haslam
**Prepress technician:** Margaret Amy Salter
**Print coordinator:** Katherine Berti

Every attempt has been made to clear copyright. Should there be any inadvertent omission please apply to the publisher for rectification.

**Picture credits:**
NASA on the Commons 6, 26, Shutterstock: Wangkun Jia 9, 12, Space Faction/Getty Images, based on NASA material 10, Shutterstock: Sunny studio 18, Shutterstock: 3Dsculptor 22.

We recommend that children are supervised at all times when using the Internet. Some of the projects in this series use a computer webcam or microphone. Please make sure children are made aware that they should only allow a computer to access the webcam or microphone on specific websites that a trusted adult has told them to use. We do not recommend children use websites or microphones on any other websites other than those mentioned in this book.

The website addresses (URLs) included in this book were valid at the time of going to press. However, it is possible that contents or addresses may have changed since the publication of this book. No responsibility for any such changes can be accepted by either the author or the Publisher.

Scratch is developed by the Lifelong Kindergarten Group at the MIT Media Lab. See http://scratch.mit.edu.

Images and illustrations from Scratch included in this book have been developed by the Lifelong Kindergarten Group at the MIT Media Lab (see http://scratch.mit.edu) and made available under the Creative Commons Attribution-ShareAlike 2.0 license (https://creativecommons.org/licenses/by-sa/2.0/deed.en). The third party trademarks used in this book are the property of their respective owners, including the Scratch name and logo. The owners of these trademarks have not endorsed, authorized, or sponsored this book.

---

**Library and Archives Canada Cataloguing in Publication**

Title: Scratch code space tech / Max Wainewright.
Other titles: Space tech
Names: Wainewright, Max, author.
Description: Series statement: Scratch code challenge | Includes index.
Identifiers: Canadiana (print) 20190107170 | Canadiana (ebook) 20190107219 | ISBN 9780778765417 (hardcover) | ISBN 9780778765691 (softcover) | ISBN 9781427123862 (HTML)
Subjects: LCSH: Astronautics—Computer programs—Juvenile literature. | LCSH: Scratch (Computer program language)—Juvenile literature. | LCSH: Computer programming—Juvenile literature.
Classification: LCC TL793 .W35 2019 | DDC j629.4—dc23

**Library of Congress Cataloging-in-Publication Data**

Names: Wainewright, Max, author.
Title: Scratch code space tech / Max Wainewright.
Other titles: Space tech
Description: New York, New York : Crabtree Publishing, 2020. | Series: Scratch code challenge | "First published in Great Britain in 2019 by Wayland." | Includes index.
Identifiers: LCCN 2019013624 (print) | LCCN 2019014505 (ebook) ISBN 9781427123862 (Electronic) | ISBN 9780778765417 (hardcover : alk. paper) | ISBN 9780778765691 (pbk. : alk. paper)
Subjects: LCSH: Astronautics--Computer programs--Juvenile literature. | Scratch (Computer program language)--Juvenile literature. | Computer programming--Juvenile literature.
Classification: LCC TL793 (ebook) | LCC TL793 .W32245 2020 (print) | DDC 629.4--dc23
LC record available at https://lccn.loc.gov/2019013624

---

**Crabtree Publishing Company**
www.crabtreebooks.com   1-800-387-7650
**Published by Crabtree Publishing Company in 2020**

Text copyright © ICT Apps, 2019
Art and design copyright © Hodder and Stoughton, 2019

All rights reserved. No part of this publication may be reproduced, stored in a retrieval system or be transmitted in any form or by any means, electronic, mechanical, photocopying, recording, or otherwise, without the prior written permission of Crabtree Publishing Company.

Printed in the U.S.A./072019/CG20190501

**Published in Canada**
Crabtree Publishing
616 Welland Ave.
St. Catharines, Ontario
L2M 5V6

**Published in the United States**
Crabtree Publishing
PMB 59051
350 Fifth Avenue, 59th Floor
New York, New York 10118

# Contents

Introduction .................................................. 4

**Project:** Blast Off! ...................................... 6

**Project:** In Control .................................... 10

**Project:** Gravity ........................................ 15

**Project:** Jetpack ....................................... 18

**Project:** Jetpack Game ............................. 21

**Project:** Satellites .................................... 22

**Project:** Return to Earth .......................... 26

Bugs and Debugging ................................. 30

Glossary ..................................................... 31

Index and Further Information ............. 32

Words in *italics* appear in the glossary on page 31.

# Introduction

In this book, we will look at some key concepts used in space technology, and explore them through coding. We will find out about *gravity* and how to deal with it and travel through space.

We'll be creating code to simulate how rockets and spaceships move. In order to experiment with the effects of gravity, we will store the value of gravity in a *variable*. By using a variable to model gravity, we will be able to make gravity stronger or weaker to see what effects it has on Earth, the Moon, and other planets.

You'll use the *algorithms* and ideas in this book (along with your imagination) to travel through space, creating your own *programs*. These programs will help you understand how space technology works, and set you on the path to dreaming up your own ideas to travel through the Universe.

There are a lot of different ways to create code. We will be using a website called Scratch to do our coding.

Type **scratch.mit.edu** into your web browser, then click Create to start a new project.

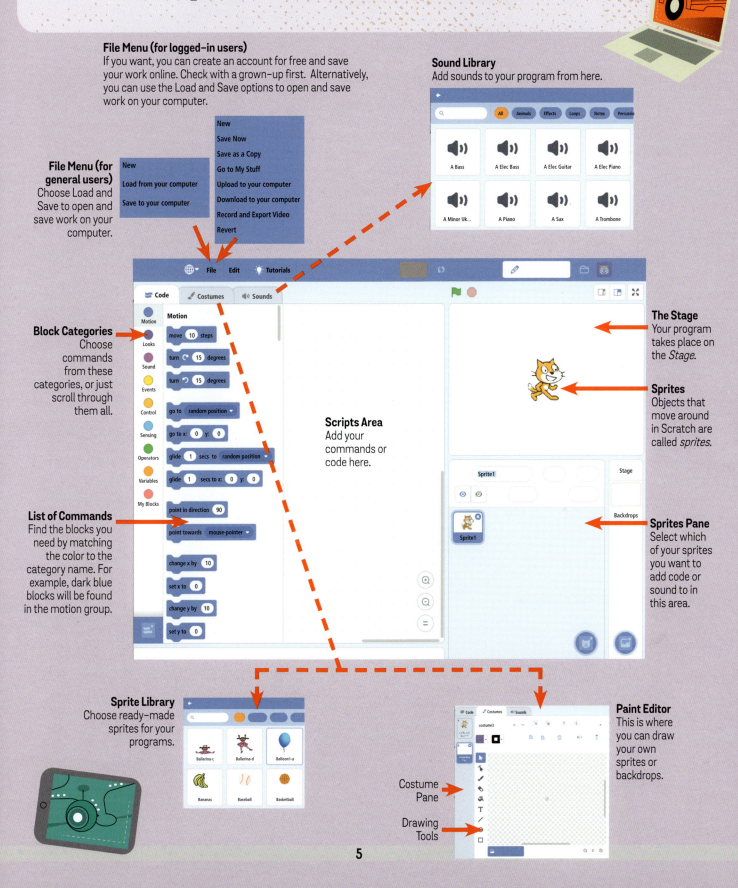

# Blast Off!

Let's start by launching a rocket into space. We'll create a simple countdown, then make our rocket move up and away.

Real rockets have to overcome gravity to take off. They do this by using very powerful engines that produce a massive amount of *thrust*.

Our program will simulate both of these forces by using a coding concept called a variable.

You'll find out more about gravity and thrust later on in this book.

### STEP 1 - **Remove the cat**

Space is no place for a cat, so *right-click* on the cat, then click **delete**.

### STEP 2 - **The backdrop**

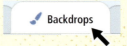

Click the **Backdrops** tab.

For help, go to: **www.maxw.com**

6

## STEP 3 – The sky

Click **Convert to Bitmap**.

Choose a light blue color.

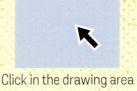
Select the **Fill** tool. Click in the drawing area to draw the sky.

Click the Undo tool if you make a mistake.

## STEP 4 – The ground

Choose a dark green color.

Select the **Rectangle** tool.

Set the rectangle to **Filled**.

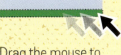
Drag the mouse to draw the ground.

## STEP 5 – Add a sprite

Click the **Choose a Sprite** button.

## STEP 6 – Add a rocket

Scroll through to find the **Rocketship**. Click on it.

## STEP 7 – How much power?

The rocket will start off with no power coming from its engines. We will then gradually increase the power until the rocket takes off. To be able to change the amount of power, we will store it in a variable. As we are dealing with rocket power, we will call the variable thrust.

Click the **Code** tab.

Click the **Variables** category.

Click **Make a Variable.**

Type **thrust**.

Click **OK**.

## STEP 8 – Gravity

Everything on Earth is affected by a force called gravity. Gravity pulls the rocket to Earth and hinders it from taking off. To simulate this in our program, we will create a variable called gravity.

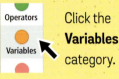  Click the **Variables** category.

Click **Make a Variable**.

Type **gravity**.

Click **OK**.

The gravity on Earth is 9.8 m/s² (meters per second squared). On other planets and their moons, the value of gravity is different.

## STEP 9 – The code

Drag the following code into the **Scripts Area**.

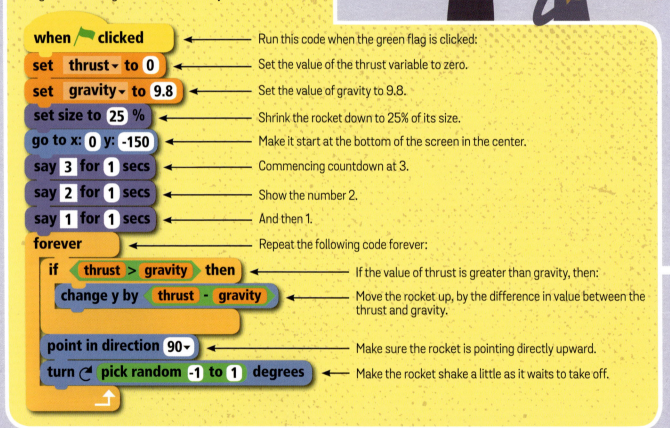

- Run this code when the green flag is clicked:
- Set the value of the thrust variable to zero.
- Set the value of gravity to 9.8.
- Shrink the rocket down to 25% of its size.
- Make it start at the bottom of the screen in the center.
- Commencing countdown at 3.
- Show the number 2.
- And then 1.
- Repeat the following code forever:
- If the value of thrust is greater than gravity, then:
- Move the rocket up, by the difference in value between the thrust and gravity.
- Make sure the rocket is pointing directly upward.
- Make the rocket shake a little as it waits to take off.

**Combining *code blocks* together:**

Start by dragging in an **if then block**.

Next, drag in a **greater than block** from the **Operators** category.

From the **Data** category, drag in a **thrust block**.

From the **Data** category, drag in a **gravity block**.

### STEP 10 – More thrust

We need to be able to increase the thrust so that the rocket takes off. Drag in another section of code to do this:

Run this code every time the space bar is pressed:

Increase the thrust by 1.

Now click the green flag to test your code.

Each time you press the space bar, the thrust value will increase. When it gets to ten, the rocket will slowly start to rise. Keep pressing it to make it accelerate.

## How it works—the rocket

Launching a rocket is a bit like letting air out of a balloon. As the air escapes out of a balloon, it pushes the balloon in the opposite direction. A rocket works in the same way, but instead of air, it blows out hot exhaust gases.

As the exhaust gases come out of the end of the rocket, they cause an equal and opposite reaction that pushes the rocket upward.

A rocket has to carry fuel and a source of oxygen so it can burn even if there is no air, as is the case in space.

## Code challenge

Make the countdown start from 5. Add a message that says "blast off" before it takes off.

Change the code to make your rocket accelerate more quickly when the space bar is pressed.

Add some code to make the rocket take off automatically.

Why not try to draw your own rocket? Click on the rocket sprite, then choose the Costumes tab. Click on the "Paint new costume" *icon* and start designing your own rocket!

# In Control

Now we have escaped from Earth's gravity and are in space! But how do we control a spaceship or rocket once it has left Earth? The rocket's main engines will keep us moving forward, but how about steering or changing course?

We will need some smaller thrusters attached to the side of the spaceship as well as the large main rocket engine. These will allow us to change direction. Let's make our own spaceship to try this.

## STEP 1 – Seeing stars

To show a dark background with stars, create a new project under the File menu.

Click on the **Stage** icon next to the **Sprites** pane.

Choose the **Backdrops** tab.

Click the **Choose a Backdrop** icon.

Click on **Stars**.

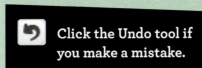 Click the Undo tool if you make a mistake.

## STEP 2 – Remove the cat

 Right-click on the cat and click **delete**.

## STEP 3 – Add a sprite

 Hover over the **Choose a Sprite** button.

 Click the **Brush** icon.

## STEP 4 – Start drawing

Start drawing the main part of the spaceship.

 Click **Convert to Bitmap**.

 Select the **Rectangle** tool.

 Set the rectangle to **Filled**.

 Choose light gray.

 Drag to create a rectangle shape, about one-third of the width of the drawing area.

## STEP 5 – Add lines

 Choose the **Line** tool.

 Pick a darker gray color.

 Make the line thicker.

 Draw two lines to make the pointed front of the spaceship.

 Pick a very dark gray color.

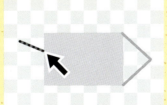 Start drawing the engine.

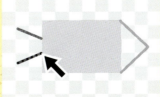 Draw a second line.

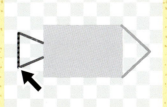 Add a final third line.

### STEP 6 – Fill in

Choose the **Fill** tool.

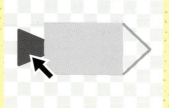

Fill the engine with color.

Select the darker gray color again.

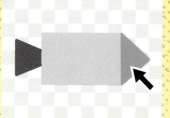

Fill in the front of the spaceship.

## How it works
### The Reaction Control System

One way to control the direction of a spaceship is to add some small additional engines called thrusters. These are like tiny rockets, one hundred times less powerful than the main engine.

The *Reaction Control System (RCS)* on this Apollo module is made from groups of four thrusters fixed to different parts of the spaceship.

Firing one of the thrusters on the left of the spaceship pushes it to the right. Firing a thruster on the right pushes the spaceship to the left.

### STEP 7 – Add a Reaction Control System

Select the **Brush** tool. Choose dark gray and make the line thicker.

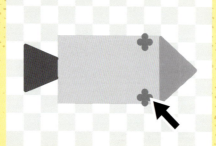

Draw a group of four thrusters on each side of the spaceship to create your RCS.

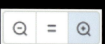

The RCS needs to be quite small. Use the zoom controls to make it easier to see what you are drawing.

> To see the main engine and RCS firing, let's add some simple animation to our program. To do this, we need to create three more pictures of the spaceship by duplicating the "costume," or the picture of the spaceship.

### STEP 8 – Simple animation

Right-click on **costume1**, under the **Costumes** tab. Then, click **duplicate**.

Repeat this step to duplicate it twice more.

You should now have four costumes of the spaceship.

### STEP 9 Main engine burn

Select **costume2**.

Use the **Brush** tool to draw flames to the main engine.

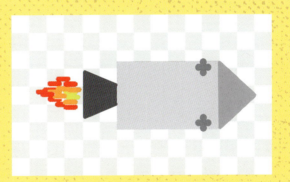

### STEP 10 – Left and right

Select **costume3**.

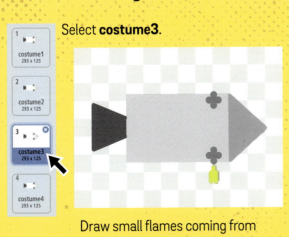

Draw small flames coming from the right side of the thruster group.

Select **costume4**.

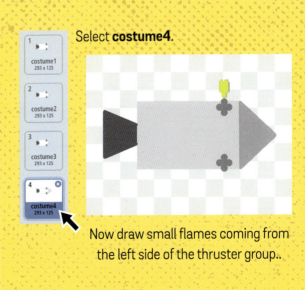

Now draw small flames coming from the left side of the thruster group..

### STEP 11 – Speed

Click the **Code** tab.

Click the **Variables** category.

Click **Make a Variable**.

Type **speed**.

Click **OK**.

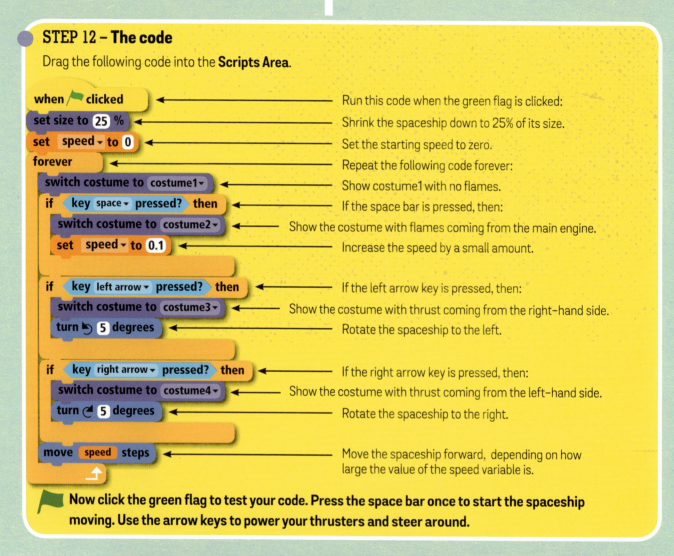

### STEP 12 – The code

Drag the following code into the **Scripts Area**.

- when flag clicked — Run this code when the green flag is clicked:
- set size to 25 % — Shrink the spaceship down to 25% of its size.
- set speed to 0 — Set the starting speed to zero.
- forever — Repeat the following code forever:
  - switch costume to costume1 — Show costume1 with no flames.
  - if key space pressed? then — If the space bar is pressed, then:
    - switch costume to costume2 — Show the costume with flames coming from the main engine.
    - set speed to 0.1 — Increase the speed by a small amount.
  - if key left arrow pressed? then — If the left arrow key is pressed, then:
    - switch costume to costume3 — Show the costume with thrust coming from the right-hand side.
    - turn ↺ 5 degrees — Rotate the spaceship to the left.
  - if key right arrow pressed? then — If the right arrow key is pressed, then:
    - switch costume to costume4 — Show the costume with thrust coming from the left-hand side.
    - turn ↻ 5 degrees — Rotate the spaceship to the right.
  - move speed steps — Move the spaceship forward, depending on how large the value of the speed variable is.

🏁 Now click the green flag to test your code. Press the space bar once to start the spaceship moving. Use the arrow keys to power your thrusters and steer around.

### Code challenge

Make the spaceship accelerate more rapidly when the space bar is pressed.

Make the spaceship turn more slowly when the left and right keys are pressed.

Make the spaceship bounce off the edge of the screen when it reaches it.

Add an extra set of thrusters to the RCS and an extra costume. Make the spaceship slow down when the "s" key is pressed.

# Gravity

Let's have a more detailed look at the force called gravity. Gravity attracts all objects toward each other. However, the effect of this force is only truly felt when one of the objects is massive. Earth's gravity is strong because Earth is much bigger than any other object nearby.

Objects on Earth are pulled toward its center by gravity. Other planets and the Moon also exert gravity. We're going to start by making a simple program that simulates how gravity works on Earth.

## STEP 1 – On Earth

Let's set the background picture to the Blue Sky background image:

Right-click on the cat and click **delete**.

Click **Choose a Backdrop**.

Click **Blue Sky**.

## STEP 2 – Gravity

We need to make a variable called gravity.

Click the **Code** tab.

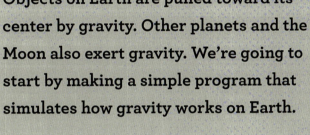

Click the **Variables** category.

Click **Make a Variable**.

Type **gravity**.

Click **OK**.

## STEP 3 – Speed

Gravity pulls falling objects toward the center of Earth. This makes falling objects accelerate. To simulate this in our program, we need to make a variable called speed.

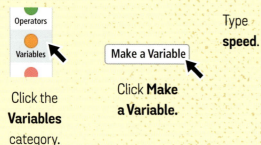

Click the **Variables** category.

Click **Make a Variable.**

Type **speed.**

Click **OK**.

## STEP 4 – Add a sprite

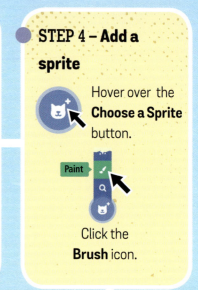

Hover over the **Choose a Sprite** button.

Click the **Brush** icon.

## STEP 5 – Draw a stick person

We need to draw a simple stick person. Start by drawing a head.

Select the **Circle** tool.

Set it to **Filled**.

Choose black.

Drag to create a circle.

> The stick person needs to be about three-quarters of the height of the drawing area. We'll shrink it with code later on.

## STEP 6 – Arms and legs

Select the line tool.

Make the line thicker.

Use the line tool to add a body, arms, and legs.

Now let's create code to make our stick person subject to the force of gravity, and see what happens!

### STEP 7 – The code

Click the **Code** tab, then drag the following code into the **Scripts Area**.

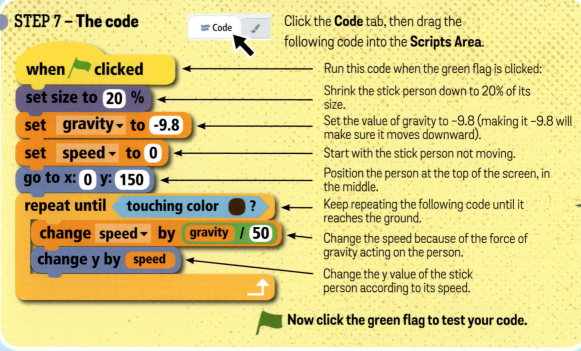

- Run this code when the green flag is clicked:
- Shrink the stick person down to 20% of its size.
- Set the value of gravity to −9.8 (making it −9.8 will make sure it moves downward).
- Start with the stick person not moving.
- Position the person at the top of the screen, in the middle.
- Keep repeating the following code until it reaches the ground.
- Change the speed because of the force of gravity acting on the person.
- Change the y value of the stick person according to its speed.

Now click the green flag to test your code.

### Setting the color

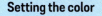 Start by clicking inside the square.

 Below the color sliders, click on the **Pipette** tool.

 Now click on the color you need on the Stage.

**Investigate**

Change the starting position for the stick person by editing the "go to x and y" values. What happens? Do they take longer to fall to Earth? Do they hit the ground as quickly?

We used −9.8 as our value for gravity. What happens if you use 9.8?

For help with combining the code blocks together, see page 8.

**Code challenge**

Create a second person to test gravity by duplicating the stick person. (Right-click on the sprite, then choose **duplicate**.) Change the starting position for the new stick person by editing the x and y values in the "go to" code block.

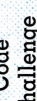

Remember, the x value tells Scratch how far across the Stage a sprite is positioned, and the y value tells it how far up the Stage.

# Jetpack

For help, go to:
www.maxw.com

**P**eople have dreamed of escaping from Earth's gravity for thousands of years. Science fiction authors have even written about personal flying machines.

One of the most exciting personal flying devices is the *jetpack*. Jetpacks are miniature rockets strapped to the wearer's back. Real jetpacks do exist now. They've been used in space, on land, and even at sea. We don't recommend you try to build your own jetpack, but you can try to create one with code.

### STEP 1 – Before you start

Make sure you have all the code from the previous three pages in your computer, and that the gravity is making your stick person fall down the screen.

### STEP 2 – Change the sprite

Click the **Costumes** tab.

### STEP 3 – Add a jetpack

Draw a simple jetpack on top of the stick person.

Select the **Rectangle** tool and set to **Filled**.

Pick a dark gray color.

Draw three rectangles to make the jetpack.

18

## STEP 4 – Add final details

Draw a jumpsuit for the stick person.

Select the **Line** tool. Choose a color.

Draw five lines to make the clothes.

Add any final details.

## STEP 5 – Duplicate

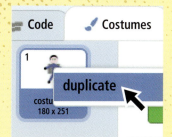

Right-click on the costume, then click **duplicate**.

Repeat this step to duplicate it again.

You should now have three copies of the costume.

## STEP 6 – Left and right

Choose **costume2**.

Use the **Brush** tool to draw flames coming from the left side of the jetpack.

Now select **costume3**.

Next, draw flames coming from the right side of the jetpack.

## STEP 7 – Left key

Click the **Code** tab, then drag the following code into the **Scripts Area**.

```
when left arrow ▼ key pressed
switch costume to costume2 ▼
turn ↻ 2 degrees
change speed ▼ by 2
```

Run this when the left arrow key is pressed:

Show the flames on the left side.

Tilt it.

Increase its speed upward.

## STEP 8 – Right key

Drag in this code for the right key:

```
when right arrow ▼ key pressed
switch costume to costume3 ▼
turn ↺ 2 degrees
change speed ▼ by 2
```

19

## STEP 9 – Main code

Edit the original code from the gravity program so it looks like this. (The first five blocks are the same. You can drag the rest of the original blocks back to the block palette.)

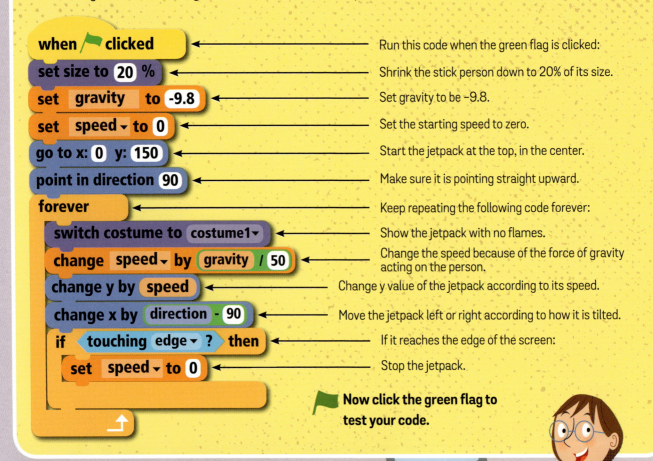

- Run this code when the green flag is clicked:
- Shrink the stick person down to 20% of its size.
- Set gravity to be –9.8.
- Set the starting speed to zero.
- Start the jetpack at the top, in the center.
- Make sure it is pointing straight upward.
- Keep repeating the following code forever:
- Show the jetpack with no flames.
- Change the speed because of the force of gravity acting on the person.
- Change y value of the jetpack according to its speed.
- Move the jetpack left or right according to how it is tilted.
- If it reaches the edge of the screen:
- Stop the jetpack.

🚩 **Now click the green flag to test your code.**

Press the left and right cursor keys quickly on the keyboard to fire the jetpack, and keep it balanced! Practice flying around the screen.

## Code challenge

Let's change our program to simulate being on the Moon.

Start by changing the backdrop to a more suitable one, such as the Moon or space.

The gravity on the Moon is 1.6 m/s². Work out how to change your code to set the value of gravity to –1.6 . You will need delicate fingers to control your jetpack in this low-gravity environment!

Find out the value of gravity on other planets and test your jetpack across the Universe.

Space

Moon

# Jetpack Game

Before you start, make sure you have a working jetpack and all the code from the last couple of pages!

We can turn the jetpack program into a simple game. The aim of the game is to collect as many rocks as possible in one minute.

## STEP 10 – The score

We need to make a variable to store the score:

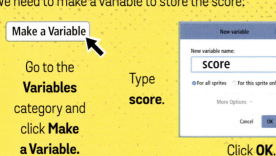

Go to the **Variables** category and click **Make a Variable**.

Type **score**.

Click **OK**.

## STEP 11 – Add a sprite

Click the **Choose a Sprite** button.

Scroll through to find the **Rocks** sprite and click on it.

## STEP 12 – Rock code

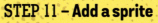

Click the **Code** tab, then drag the following code into the **Scripts Area**.

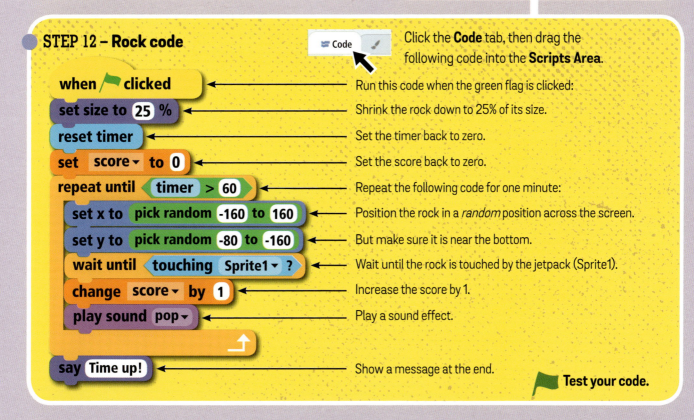

- when 🏁 clicked — Run this code when the green flag is clicked:
- set size to 25 % — Shrink the rock down to 25% of its size.
- reset timer — Set the timer back to zero.
- set score to 0 — Set the score back to zero.
- repeat until timer > 60 — Repeat the following code for one minute:
  - set x to pick random -160 to 160 — Position the rock in a *random* position across the screen.
  - set y to pick random -80 to -160 — But make sure it is near the bottom.
  - wait until touching Sprite1? — Wait until the rock is touched by the jetpack (Sprite1).
  - change score by 1 — Increase the score by 1.
  - play sound pop — Play a sound effect.
- say Time up! — Show a message at the end.

🏁 **Test your code.**

# Satellites

A *satellite* is something that *orbits* a planet. The Moon is a natural satellite. There are also thousands of artificial satellites in orbit around Earth.

Satellites are used for all kinds of purposes, including communication and navigation. Satellite navigation (satnav) devices, for example, use satellites to find where we are. They are also used to study space and Earth, and to predict the weather.

● **STEP 1 – Stars**

Let's start by picking a dark background with nothing but stars.

Right-click on the cat, then click **delete**.

Click on the **Stage** icon next to the **Sprites** pane.

Click the **Choose a Backdrop** icon.

Click on **Stars**.

Normally, moving objects want to keep moving in a straight line (this is called momentum). But the force of gravity also pulls a satellite back toward Earth. When the two forces of momentum and gravity are balanced, the satellite travels around Earth in a curved path called an orbit.

● **STEP 2 – The Earth**

Click the **Choose a Sprite** button. Scroll through to find **Earth** and click on it.

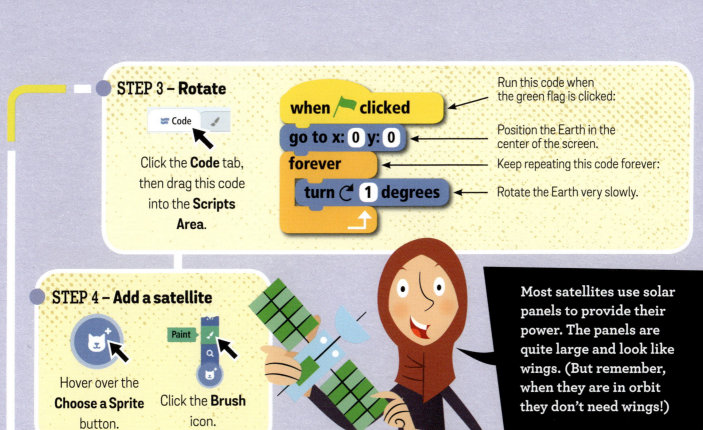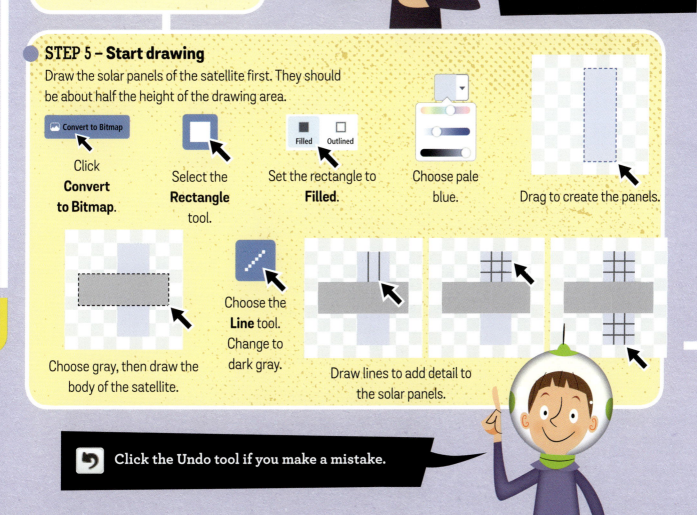

## STEP 6 – Speed variable

Create a variable to store the speed of the satellite.

Click the **Variables** category.

Click **Make a Variable**.

Type **speed**.

Click **OK**.

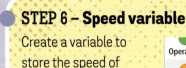
Click the **Code** tab.

## STEP 7 – The code

Drag this code into the **Scripts Area** to make the satellite orbit the Earth.

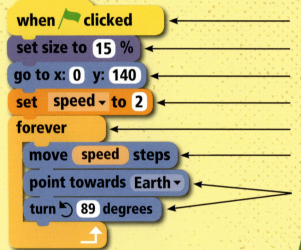

Run this code when the green flag is clicked:

Shrink the satellite down to 15% of its size.

Start it in the center of the screen near the top.

Set its speed to 2.

Repeat the following code forever:

Move it forward according to its speed.

These two blocks of code simulate gravity pulling the satellite toward Earth, and its momentum keeping it moving forward.

🚩 **Now click the green flag to test your code.**

The Earth should slowly spin, and the satellite should orbit around it. (Because we aren't using 3-D images, the Earth will turn clockwise rather than rotate the way it really does.)

Now we will turn our satellite into a communications satellite. It will simulate sending messages down to Earth and back.

## STEP 8 – Add another sprite

Click the **Choose a Sprite** button.

Scroll through to find the **Ball** and click on it.

## STEP 9 – Communication code

This code will simulate a radio signal being transmitted back and forth between Earth and the satellite. Drag it into the **Scripts Area**.

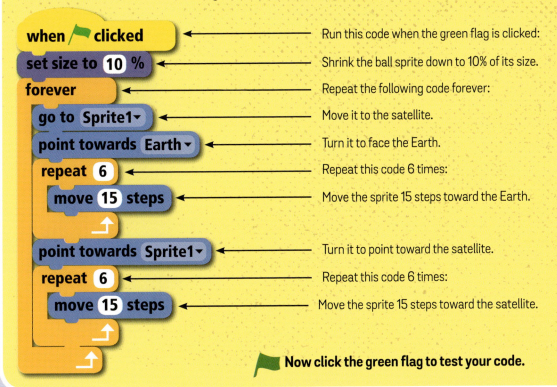

- when 🏳 clicked — Run this code when the green flag is clicked:
- set size to 10 % — Shrink the ball sprite down to 10% of its size.
- forever — Repeat the following code forever:
  - go to Sprite1 — Move it to the satellite.
  - point towards Earth — Turn it to face the Earth.
  - repeat 6 — Repeat this code 6 times:
    - move 15 steps — Move the sprite 15 steps toward the Earth.
  - point towards Sprite1 — Turn it to point toward the satellite.
  - repeat 6 — Repeat this code 6 times:
    - move 15 steps — Move the sprite 15 steps toward the satellite.

🏳 Now click the green flag to test your code.

## Investigate

Try changing the value in the set size code blocks. What happens?

Change the amount turned in the turn counterclockwise code block for the satellite. Try using 80 instead of 89 degrees. What happens? Try using a larger number.

## Code challenge

Try changing the value of the satellite's speed variable from 2 to a slightly smaller or larger value. Can you make the satellite stay over one part of the Earth and rotate at the same speed as the Earth? This is called a geostationary satellite.

Create a second satellite by duplicating the first one. Change its code to make sure it starts in a different place.

# Return to Earth

Rockets and spaceships are usually built from separate modules or parts.

Only some parts of a spaceship return to Earth. The Apollo space missons used *parachutes* to slow down the Command Module (CM) on its return to Earth. The CM brought astronauts back from space and splashed down into the ocean. Let's recreate this with code.

### STEP 1 – The ocean and sky

Let's start by drawing the ocean and the sky.

Right-click on the cat, then click **delete**.

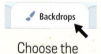

Choose the **Backdrops** tab.

### STEP 2 – Start drawing

Start with the ocean.

Click **Convert to Bitmap**.

Choose the **Rectangle** tool.

Set to **Filled**.

Pick turquoise for the ocean.

Drag to create a thin rectangle shape at the bottom of the screen.

### STEP 3 – Blending colors

We need to create a sky that is black at the edge of space, fading through to blue below.

Select the **Fill** tool.

Choose black.

Select the **Down Gradient** option.

Now pick dark blue as the second color.

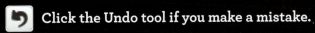 Click the Undo tool if you make a mistake.

## STEP 4 – The sky

Click to color in the sky.

## STEP 5 – Add a sprite

Hover over the **Choose a Sprite** button.

Click the **Brush** icon.

## STEP 6 – Draw the Command Module

 Choose the **Line** tool.

 Make the line thicker.

 Choose light gray.

Draw a triangle.

Select the **Fill** tool.

Fill the Command Module with color.

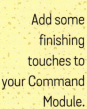
Add some finishing touches to your Command Module.

## STEP 7 – Duplicate

We need to draw a second version of the Command Module, with a parachute. Remember, Scratch calls this second picture a costume.

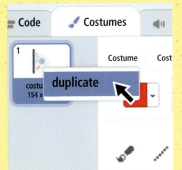

Right-click on the **Costume** icon, then click **duplicate**.

A copy of the costume should appear.

Once our returning Command Module gets close to Earth, gravity will start to make it fall very quickly. We will need to add a parachute to reduce the effect of gravity, and allow it to land more slowly.

## STEP 8 – Draw the parachute

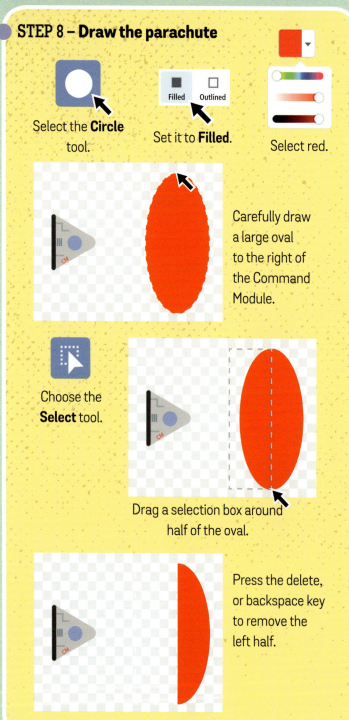

Select the **Circle** tool.

Set it to **Filled**.

Select red.

Carefully draw a large oval to the right of the Command Module.

Choose the **Select** tool.

Drag a selection box around half of the oval.

Press the delete, or backspace key to remove the left half.

## STEP 9 – Attach it

Choose the **Line** tool.

Pick dark gray.

Make the line thicker.

Draw some ropes to connect the parachute.

## STEP 10 – The code

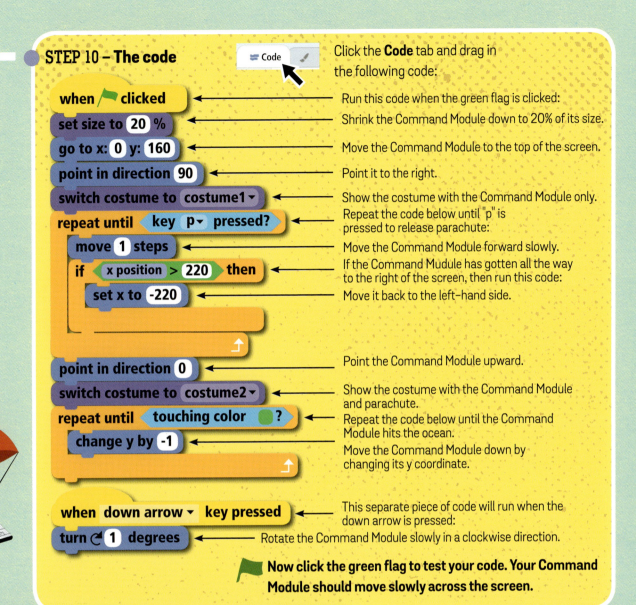

Click the **Code** tab and drag in the following code:

- Run this code when the green flag is clicked:
- Shrink the Command Module down to 20% of its size.
- Move the Command Module to the top of the screen.
- Point it to the right.
- Show the costume with the Command Module only.
- Repeat the code below until "p" is pressed to release parachute:
- Move the Command Module forward slowly.
- If the Command Mudule has gotten all the way to the right of the screen, then run this code:
- Move it back to the left-hand side.
- Point the Command Module upward.
- Show the costume with the Command Module and parachute.
- Repeat the code below until the Command Module hits the ocean.
- Move the Command Module down by changing its y coordinate.
- This separate piece of code will run when the down arrow is pressed:
- Rotate the Command Module slowly in a clockwise direction.

🏁 **Now click the green flag to test your code. Your Command Module should move slowly across the screen.**

Press the down arrow to slowly aim the Command Module towards the ocean. When the Command Module is low enough, press the "p" key to release the parachute. It should then gently glide down to the ocean.

## Investigate

What happens if you change the 220 and –220 values in the "if" code block? What are the best values for your Command Module to use?

## Code challenge

The parachute should slow the Command Module down considerably. Change the code to make it fall even more slowly.

If the Command Module enters the atmosphere at too steep an angle it will get hot and could burn up. Add some code that checks to see if the angle is more than 105 degrees and gives a warning message. It should also stop the program.

# Bugs and debugging

If you find your code isn't working as expected, stop and look through each command you selected. Think about what you want it to do, and what it is really telling the computer to do. If you are creating one of the programs in this book, check that you have not missed a line. Some things to check:

**Join block properly:**

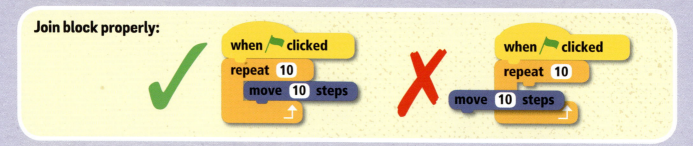

**Select sprites before adding code:**

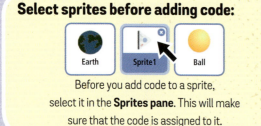

Before you add code to a sprite, select it in the **Sprites pane**. This will make sure that the code is assigned to it.

**X or Y?**

y Don't mix them up!
→ x

**The right size**

A sprite that is the wrong size may stop your code from working. Use the squares as a guide when drawing sprites. You can always use the set size % value to make them fit properly.

**Right color, wrong code?**

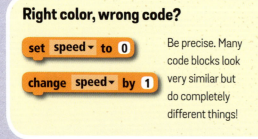

Be precise. Many code blocks look very similar but do completely different things!

**Position variables and values carefully:**

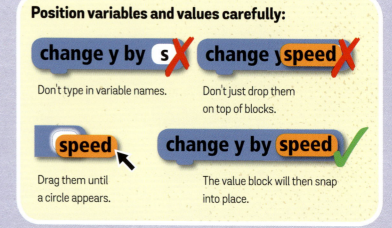

Don't type in variable names.

Don't just drop them on top of blocks.

Drag them until a circle appears.

The value block will then snap into place.

**Tips to reduce *bugs*:**
- When things are working properly, spend time looking through your code so you understand each line.

Experiment and change your code. Try out different values.
To be good at *debugging*, you need to understand what each code block does and how your code works.

- Practice debugging! Make a very short program and get a friend to change one block only, while you aren't looking. Can you fix it?
- If you are making your own program, spend time drawing a diagram and planning it before you start. Try changing values if things don't work, and don't be afraid to start again—you will learn from it.

# Glossary

| | |
|---|---|
| algorithm | Rules or steps used to make something work or complete a task |
| bug | An error in a program that stops it from working properly |
| code block | A draggable instruction icon used in Scratch |
| debug | To remove bugs (or errors) from a program |
| degrees | The units used to measure angles |
| gravity | A force that pulls objects together. It is only noticeable if one of the objects is massive, such as a planet. |
| icon | A small, clickable image on a computer |
| jetpack | A complex low-powered rocket system worn on your back |
| orbit | The circular path taken by one object, often around a larger object |
| parachute | A device that slows down a falling object by using air resistance |
| program | A set of coded instructions for a computer |
| random | A number that can't be predicted |
| Reaction Control System (RCS) | A group of thrusters working together to steer a spaceship |
| right-click | To click the right mouse button |
| satellite | An object (for example, a communications device) that orbits around another object, such as a planet |
| sprite | An object with a picture on it that moves around the stage |
| stage | The place in Scratch that sprites move around |
| steps | Small movements made by sprites |
| thrust | The force that pushes something along, for example, a rocket's engines |
| variable | Part of a program that stores a value that can change |

# Index and Further Information

**A**
animation 13

**B**
backdrops 5–6, 10, 15, 20, 22, 26
bugs 30

**C**
color, adding 7, 11–12, 16, 18–19, 23, 26–28
command blocks 5, 8–9, 14, 17, 19–21, 23–25, 29–30
coordinates (x, y) 8, 17, 20–21, 23–24, 29–30
costumes 9, 13–14, 18–20, 27

**D**
debugging 30
drawing 5, 7, 9, 11–13, 16, 18–19, 23, 26–28

**G**
gravity 4, 6, 8, 10, 15–20, 22, 24, 28

**J**
jetpack game 21
jetpacks 18–20

**M**
momentum 22, 24

**P**
parachutes 26–29

**R**
Reaction Control System 12–14
rocket, launching a 4, 6–9

**S**
satellites 22–25
sprite, adding a 5, 7, 9, 11, 16, 21–24, 27, 30

**T**
thrust 6–9
thrusters 10–14

**V**
variables 4, 6–8, 14–16, 21, 24–25, 30

### FURTHER INFORMATION

Gifford, Clive. *Awesome Algorithms and Creative Coding.* Crabtree Publishing Company, 2015.

Wainewright, Max. *I'm a Scratch Coder.* Crabtree Publishing Company, 2018.

Woodcock, Jon. *Coding Projects in Scratch.* 2nd Edition. DK Children, 2019.
London, UK: 2017.